Welcome To Hell

(And Other Poems About Adulthood)

Liam Xavier

Book Cover Design by Sigourney Whitesel

www.liamxavier.co.uk
www.sigourneywhiteselstudio.com

ISBN: 978-1-8380271-0-0

This is not a pessimistic book.

While the title may lead you to believe we are about to embark on a journey of anger and angst, heartbreak and pain, this book is all about optimism.

Some days it can feel like adulthood is the literal definition of Hell. The fiery pits, the never-ending torture, the repetition of mistakes and the undying feeling that we are going nowhere. BUT we all know it's actually about growth.
We are not sitting in the proverbial death chambers, we are at the start of our lives and we are discovering who we are. Which some might say is the same. But it's not, I promise.

If you stick with me, you'll see what I mean. From the first poem to the last, we will look at the worst and the best and understand that its all part of the journey.

Contents

The Fear						*5*

The Contradiction				*23*

The Clarity						*69*

Thank You For Reading				*115*

The Fear

Welcome To Hell

"Welcome to Hell!" is what I tell myself as the clock
signals it is my 20th birthday.

The 1st April - already a joke.

It does not matter how horrendous I found my teenage
years, this will be the decade to end it all, I'm sure.

This will be the independence I was never ready for.

This will be the worst thing physically possible.

Twenty. It even sounds terrifying. Twenty.

"You're still a baby" the elders tell me.

Well yes, in comparison, I'm sure that is correct but I
feel like a baby with every wrinkle possible if I
am.

Am I being too dramatic?

I am a performer, or I was in my former, non-elderly
state for I am now the old man with the walker, the
stuttered talker, the mumbling moaner.

Maybe I am being dramatic after all.

Oh god, my career - I don't have one.
It's too late, I'll never make anything of myself.

I'm nearly thirty now, which means I'm nearly fifty,

Fuck I'm screwed up.

Twenty.

It doesn't even make sense, I was a mere child just a day ago and now I already feel like I have a thousand debts, a mortgage, a pension, and do I even have to mention the fact I can already feel my back crippling under the pain of my old age?

Perhaps I am being a little over-dramatic.

I guess we will have to see, but I cannot help this hellish fear that overwhelms as I count the candles on the cake and watch my innocence fade away.

I wonder if I'll survive this ride.

Beginnings.

There is something about you that lingers.

Maybe,
it is the subtle conversation you make,
or the breaths you steal away
with the shape your figure creates when you walk
closer,
trying not to make it too obvious that you want to be
near, amongst a new and thrilling atmosphere.

Maybe
it is your eyes in the corner of mine, staring,
wondering whether to speak,
there is something unique in you,
that lingers.

Maybe
it is my youth that cannot see the truth
that I am just a little lonely and see love
where I need it to be or

Maybe
it is the smooth texture of your voice
the noise your silence leaves, so unwelcome,
please
keep talking to me,
i do not want to see

you leave me now
til i can find a way to continue this
beginning.
With carefully collected words
and stolen songs from passing birds,
have you ever heard the tale
of two lovers who said goodbye
without a hint to try?

Maybe,
we will reminisce upon this moment,
this meeting
that lingers the way you linger on my mind.
This moment where two lovers could read the faces
of the other, covered in truth
and be soothed by the way
they could sit beside each other
and speak as if lovers from birth.

Maybe,
I have just been reading too many lovesick poems
and I cannot escape their fantasies
and you do not see me the same
but wouldn't it be something
to find out?

Late Buses

I could see you in the corner of my eyes.
A girl I had seen so many times before,
but never thought to talk to,
and yet, to the side of my eyes.

I see you try,
I see your stares,
I see you move closer,

I wonder if you will say Hello,
if I will be brave enough to keep conversation,
and then you utter words to me in casual chatter,
a musing on the lateness of our bus,
the whole reason we have met.
I laugh and you sit next to me,
I can feel our breaths, and think of something to say,
before I know it we are talking like new friends,
we sigh and share a laugh as the bus finally pulls near,
and then when you eventually leave before me,
turn to me, as you get up and say goodbye,
I am sad to see you leave.

What if we have our one chance in the whole world
and cannot get it back?

Passerby.

I found a window to stare out of,
somewhere in the back of a dim lit cafe
with the smell of wasted coffee
from everyone rushing to work.
I sat and thought of all the people outside,
kissing couples
and others waving goodbye,
What are they saying?
Is it love?
Is it touch?
Is it pain?
Is it feigned?
I need to know,
there is just something so frustrating
about watching them go
and never knowing
what happens to their story.

Where?

Once my teeth have no nails left to bite,
once my hands are bored of pulling at my hair,
once the scratching does not satisfy the distraction,
once the tired is the angry is the sad is the empty,
staring at what is left,
hovering between the cliff edge,
and its fall,
I whisper in the wind,
lost in the winter.
Words are not the same,
the whisper is not mine,
the vision is not in sight,
just twists and locks,
and the emblem of a key,
taunting my peripheral,
and the man behind the door
is not me,
and the door is not locked,
its wide open,
and I cannot find the good
in the padlock or the welcome sign,
so where do I go from here?

Loneliness

Tonight feels like my bedroom stands
detached atop the worlds surface.
I dare not open my door for fear that I might fall out,
so I sit on my double bed
that feels double the double it already is,
like I could roll over and over
and still be in the centre
and I wonder if anyone is shouting up to me,
trying to arrange a miracle to bring me back into
society.
Because if they are, their voices must be lost in the
distance, because all I can hear
is quiet, not to be confused with tranquillity,
quiet, so silent I have to pinch my skin
to see if I am still alive,
or the only one left.
But my screen still lights up, voices typed,
company of sorts,
but this is emotional not physical,
and even if everyone in the world were in this room of
mine,
there would still be a whisper of doubt.
A slither of silence cutting my throat,
a double vision visualising their distaste for me.
What a sharp knife is loneliness
in the presence of so much love.

Losing

Nothing happens to the sky.
The seasons change all the same;
The sun is bright of a day, and hidden of another.
But gradually, my life has fallen down
a spiralling path
and I am afraid I might just lose it all.
I trusted in his words, and then he used new ones
to sever my heart.
I believed her love and then she stole mine for its parts
and left only the rotten pieces.
I heard my voice and then it changed and I could no
longer recognise its wave.
What would be the next journey for me?
Could I survive?
Would anything remain?
Or would the pain be the final straw?

I'm Starting To Understand Bukowski

What a miserable man that Charles was.
At least that is what I first thought when my eyes
were drawn to the words of that large headed,
wrinkled man we read about in class.

That tone so low and raspy, a throat telling a story of a
lifetime of mistreatment, and debauchery.

That face - Old, even when it wasn't.
That poetry - So pessimistic and slow.

That was another thing, you could never read a
Bukowski poem fast. It had to be done with intent
with the slur of a drunk and the pace of a pensioner.

And yet, I could not stop reading on and have not yet.
In fact, I'm starting to understand the old cynic.
I am barely a quarter of my life old and still his words
are beginning to ring true.

The cursing of the world, the deprecation of the self,
the pain in reflection. Oh, you see he was so broken
and so problematic, but in his ageing ways, I feel I can
see the person he always wanted to be.

I have changed my mind

After a time tied to one vision of my future,
I have changed my mind
and there seems to be nothing scarier.

There is comfort in being so sure of your path,
I wanted to act, to take to the stage and screen
but now I have fallen out of love with the journey
and the pen is a mightier passion now.

But what if such a change so far in is a devastating
one?
What if there is no way back?
What if I have misjudged these talents and I cannot
make it?

What if? What if? Give me some certainty.

I have changed my mind and to make matters worse
I do not think this will be the last time.
So I guess I will remain in fear of my choices
and keep finding out if they were worth it.

The Gull

There were boats on the rivers when the birds flocked
for summer.

I saw one steal a sandwich from someone on board.
It flew and flew and dropped the sandwich like
garbage
and I could not help but stifle a nervous kind of
laughter.

The Sun

There is always a fear I have of the sun;
thickening air perfecting its grip on my throat,
rays of a weatherly glaze over the earth
that burns my skin
and the feeling of not caring of its scorn
so long as I feel its warmth.

I do not want to get used to its summery sheen
lest it leaves too quickly and the winter freezes me
by surprise.

I fear the sun because I never expect it to stay long,
and it hurts less to avoid it than to accept it in the
moment.

I can but I cannot.

I can whistle, but not very melodically.
I can sing, but not terribly well.

And I can dream of you,
but I cannot make it real.

Losing Friends

I do not want to lose any more friends
but life sure does love to take them from me.
I am always left cleaning off the shadows
on my heart and it is never a quiet process.
So do not be so surprised
when I plead you to never leave.

The Contradiction

In Love

I'm always nervous to write about love,
because I don't know much about it,
no,
I don't know much about people,
no,
I don't know much about myself
in love,
not really.

I know that my heart beats that rhythm
that I lose all my senses and become devoted
to the notion of a future with someone
but I just end up, in love or not,
putting pen to paper and making these sonnets.

You see in love, I would turn to you,
sometimes a bumbling mess,
sometimes perfectly normal,
but dreaming of your hands in mine,
and our minds intertwined,
sometimes I have a little too much wine,
and I let my fingers do their little dance
across my phone,
threatening the safety of a secret.
I've done this more than once over many years,
I fall,
I infatuate,

I wait
the bubble rises and I see your face everywhere,
that's how it goes
and who knows maybe the pavement will stop
dragging me under
when my heart is too heavy for my chest.
Or maybe it will swallow me whole
when it smells the passion in my soul,
and I know it sounds so dramatic,
but its like I'm a fanatic for you
whoever you are at the time,
blonde hair and green eyes,
or black hair and on the rise,
too wise for the world
or too timely for me.
Because it seems
the seconds, the minutes, are just a little off a lot
and what I'm saying,
is I don't know what I'm doing half the time.
I whistle and I rhyme and sometimes search for signs
but I find that just prolongs everything.
I'm just a little awkward,
just a little misled, mistrusting
missing too many people to ever make this easy,
but I promise whoever you are
whoever you will be,
you will be loved,
by the man in the glasses
standing too tall for his clumsiness,

and thinking of ways to make you happy
so that you'll never find a reason to leave him,
what I am trying to say is
whoever you are,
whoever you will be,
you will be loved.

R.

I have spent the majority of my life hoping I would
never meet you again
but there are days when all I crave is to sit you down,
and look you in the eyes,
and tell you everything I have harboured
and make you listen
to every single life-locked word,
every nightmare I survived,
every night-time regression,
and just watch those callous eyes,
dead inside,
because even when I have tried
to forget, your memory keeps coming back
like a silhouette tainting the sunlight.
And sometimes I wonder
if it would even hurt you a little
to hear my words,
if you would even bat your eyelids in shame.

And then I sit back, grow older and realise,
it would make no difference
and I am better without knowing.

Remember who you are.

I lose myself in the pictures eye,
But I'll never be what the camera feeds,
dwarfed and distorted,
in real life,
what am I,
but nothing?

Nothing? Nothing? You are everything.

I have killed my heart,
stitches and open wounds,
scabs that won't heal,
am I destined to bleed?
Destined to feel?
I would rather
the veins and nerves under my skin,
popped and left me without a name.

You have strength in you.
There is love, and power and choice.
You have to trust yourself.

Trusting myself is not a luxury
I can afford to believe in.

Smile

The smile is a grand thing.
I wear it often;
sometimes with teeth
and a head jerk backward
but I have become exceptionally
good at wearing it
without the truth;
so regularly in fear of it, in fact.
Desperation is a smile.
Suicide is a smile.
Heartache is a smile.
HelpMe is a smile.
I'mHurting is a smile.
Idon'tKnowHowToTellYou is a smile.
What is rarely just a smile … is a smile.

Sleep

Morning arrives,
like a tide washing ashore,
the aftermath of a tsunami,
the calm left by destruction,
nothing but a soft percussion,
a hi hat tapping in the back of the mind.

What an anti-climax sleep has created,
just yesterday the thunder was so loud
it could have crashed through my skull,
and now, not even a drizzle of rain,
just a sky of sun and a head full of shame.
I climbed the mountain
just to jump off the top
and land on clouds
made of excuses to justify,
and to think if I just applied
all the methods my friends teach me,
it would all be so easy
or so you would imagine.

Each night, my eyes close,
I alight from my caffeine high
to arrive at a dream or a nightmare,
or simply a transition
from day to next day,
hoping this will be the one.

If I could start again,
I wouldn't,
because look at everything I've learnt,
from heroes, and friends and mistakes made,
this is not how you play the game,
you cannot fall over and die
and press the start button
to bring up a menu to begin all over again,
there is no pause,
no fast forward,
no quick clothes change,
and if you hurt someone,
it does not just log on your console
as a bonus,
you just have to take the hit
you have to take the loss,
and you can sleep away the day,
and say you don't care,
but you don't wear your scars as trophies,
you wear them as nothing.
Be proud,
wake up,
sleep is your healer
only if your eyes open.
I am old for my age,
because I have aged in experience,
the way a phone ages after it has been dropped so
many times,
I am bruised and damaged, and sometimes I do not

work the way I should,
but I am still strong,
and know more than I probably should,
and my mind is a childs see-saw,
without much balance.

I wake one morning bright and alive,
and before I fall to my slumber that evening,
my energy will be gone
and the ceiling will become the watch
dangled loosely by a questionable therapist,
hypnotised,
drowned in lies,
trying to listen to the wise.
We are all a mess,
neatly organised,
in a circle just tight enough
to help us survive in the presence of each other
there is no answer to any one question,
there is sleep
there is love,
there is beauty
there is friendship,
there is you,
listening to you
and your needs.
This may sound somewhat melancholic,
but I hear the orchestra creeping through the cracks,
every time my eyes want to sing their little tune of

solitude,
and it is beautiful,
the horns,
the trumpets,
they sound
when the noise is too loud,
and you need the moments
to reflect
in retrospect
without fear that it is too late,
darling,
sleep a night,
and start again.

Tonight, I feel unlovable.

Tonight I feel unlovable; the troublesome burden who
does not know how to turn the temporary to
permanent.
I am fervently frightened of falling apart.
It is like a passion to peer into my future,
escape from here and paint the scene of a dream life;
the kids,
the wife,
the cottage with the typewriter.

I feel unlovable, still.

Even with all my hope and will,
I am yet to feel totally wanted
and not because I am not
but because I am terrified of believing it.

I feed the fear, as I grieve the peers
that have left me, the rest who got bored
or could not afford me their patience any more.

Because I am no longer the child or the teen
searching for a team of friends and loves
and holding so desperately on.
I was so broken then but now so
many have gone without warning,
and I am left wondering if I have the capability

to be loved in the long run.

I feel unlovable like I am the dispensable love listed in
some book for sad boys who make the perfect
substitute spouse, but only until they stop feeling
lonely and I am the only one left with love on my lips.

I feel unlovable but I am old enough to know my
feelings are not always truthful.

And the healing will come and I will be the hapless
human holding hearts and hearing their parts sing
my name.

I will be the friend, the love that accepts when another
tells me they love me and they need me.

Until then, I will keep loving them and working on my
self and my own health, for there is little else that will
help.

Goodnight.

If there is one thing I both hate and love about being a
grown up, it is that I can accept this is over.

If I was younger, I might have the hunger for hope,
like the only way to cope would be me lying to myself.

Dreams and schemes of how I could change time, until
things were fine and you were finally mine.
But I have grown.
I could never have known you would be the one to
talk of love and then leave.
I want you to call me and speak in apologetic tones
and tell me how I am your only home.
I know it is just lies.
I do not want any of those things.

I just miss you. I just miss being your friend. I still
wish you the best health but I am ready to walk on, so
please don't talk me out of it.

Don't call, I am afraid I might pick up.

Alone

I am learning how to be alone again;
I find I do it every once or twice a year and I do it
slowly and with reluctance.
The breathing steadies itself gradually.
The necessity for the company of a human subsides.
The mandatory music to disguise the silence becomes
optional and that old dream of spending a moment in
an old cottage in the south of France, typing away at
my novel, returns.

Oh, to dream of solitude when love still exists is a
freeing thing.

Seeking.

I have been searching for something without a name
for too long. With no face and no body, I have chased
it to the edges of the earth and nearly fallen off. Some
days I believe it speaks to me; a crisp whisper in times
of sadness, but I can never quite trace it back.

A woman, perhaps? The feeling of companionship; to
love and walk the streets hand-in-hand and fight over
meagre issues solved in communication.

A job, perhaps? Something new to ignite the senses, a
venture never before taken.

A flight, perhaps? Across the pond or on the other side
of the world; an escape to anywhere on the map.

No, I don't believe it is any of those.

To see a woman as the answer would be to do a
disservice to such a woman. To strike a selfish love
made from my inability to define purpose would be
nothing short of a subconscious manipulation.

A job can change things but I am happy in mine, if I
were to move, I would move into another career with
just as strong a frown.

And a flight? Well yes, it is good for distraction
and perhaps I might even find the 'thing' I am seeking
but it would not be the thing itself.

I don't think it is quite so simple.

I think it comes in waves of feeling.

Feeling that comes when you are not searching for it.

A simplicity that is complex in other ways and cannot
be chased.

I do not know what the thing is, but I will leave a
space for it for when it is ready to arrive.

Nap-time.

I have found that most things we are taught in
childhood
are completely useless in adulthood,
except maybe that a nap in the daytime
can sometimes make a world of difference.

You could be unstoppable.

Do not listen to expectations,
but rather the imagination of your heart.

When I Met You

I have come to the conclusion,
through many mishaps of my adult life,
that I am inherently attracted to
anyone who bears their soul in vulnerability
and accepts mine in the same state
and I think I have been mistaking that
for love -
so much so that I'm no longer sure of
what any of it means,
and for the time being,
I think I will merely love,
just with a little extra caution,
no restrictions,
no pressure,
just caution.

The Same Care

I have spent a long time telling others
to develop their own flowers of belief
and to accept better love from others
and I think,
only just now am I doing the same
for myself - finally.

At Least

She was my final wake up call,
and though she no longer makes a sound,
like a rooster at dawn,
I still open my eyes
to a new day
with purpose.

Shock.

What is this electricity?
Every time I try to touch it,
It gives me quite the shock,
have you felt it before?
Can you disarm it?
Or must we take the tremor
to reach the safety?
I am just a little too tired
of running from such things.

A Sonnet To Lovesick Poets

Is this not the most complicated life?
Thinking that love like sonnets true is dead?
Control the feeling that sharpens the knife
or else watch, again, the devil be fed.
The words do come easier than action.
So we see poets lives hidden in black
scattered talk of a new lovesick faction,
we belong to song, hidden from attack.
Maybe blue was the wrong colour to say,
When the sky is falling under large hearts,
more appropriate would be a fine grey.
We are drowning but still we make our art,
no words take the place of the love we've known.
But with these pen licked tears, my, how we've grown.

How I've survived

Sometimes survival means a book of scribbles
written in the cold quiet early hours of the restless
morning.

Sometimes it is mumblings that are never shared.

Sometimes it is mumblings that someone trained
translates to epiphanies to make the brain clearer.

Sometimes it is just believing that survival is on the
cards, and you must play as many rounds as it takes to
get the perfect hand.

The truth is, I don't know how I've survived, but I do
know I can do it again and again so long as I try.

Nice Guy

I like to think I am a nice guy.

I was raised to be polite, to treat people with kindness
and stay away from fights.
But what I have realised, from years of being a 'nice
guy' is that there are rules to this thing.

It is not the same stupid songs you hear of no-one
being attracted to a 'nice guy' or those that say a 'nice
guy' can never be respected.

It is one and only one
essential guideline: take care of yourself the same.

If you live like this and want to help.
If you look after others and not yourself,
you are doing it all wrong.

To be a nice guy is treat others with respect, to take
every day as a chance to place a smile on a face but if,
in doing so, you take that smile away from your own,
things must change.

The simple equation for being a 'nice guy' is that you
love who you are enough to share that brightness with
others.

Ambiguous

Ambiguous,
skin of colour,
tone unknown.
The boy ambiguous
searches for a home
but never knows who to call.
White says one,
black says another,
why does it matter?
Says the other.
He ponders the last question
as if it were a parable,
as if his conflicts
were not born of him.
But he knows so long as
the contradiction shows
in the shape of his nose
and the colour of his hair
against its texture,
he must understand the basis
of their stares.
He learns in school, in college, in university
of the adversity his ancestors survived
of the equalities for which they died
and more, as the days go by, he realises
he cannot handle his race with the same erasure
history has for centuries.

He is the empire and the slave.
He is the abolishment and the beauty,
the creolisation and the patience of strength.
He is mixed.
He is not a side to be picked
or a field of cotton.
He is not the ruler
or devoid of privilege.
He is mixed.
He passes,
he teaches himself outside of his classes,
the histories of identity,
the world's propensity for denial
in the form of guilt.
He is mixed.
He is proud.
He will name his heritage loud
and he will not let you
decide the outcome
of his own fight of a lifetime.

Evidence.

I had not noticed,
until the sun began to light the sky,
just how dirty my glasses had gotten.
A few wisps of eyelash,
some sprinkles of dust
and a scattering of sleep.
I clean them every half hour on average.
It is astonishing how quickly the dust gathers.
Oh and the scratch - Where did that come from?
and another hair, trapped in the metal hinge,
but it is the wrong colour to be mine.
It stretches as it pulls, light and long and harsh.
Oh, the sunshine spotlights the stray frayed hair -
the last remaining evidence.

Oh, how the dust still gathers after the winter is done.

None

No solution solves my delusion
And so I will love you on my own forever,
In some secretive corner in my brain.
I wonder if I will try to deny it
a year or two down the line.
I wonder if I will mean it.

A Painful Year

I am struggling to find a reason to thank the year for
its lessons
but perhaps I will find it after midnight in a drunken
stupor,
with kissing strangers behind me,
my friends in front of me
and a gin fizz in my hand.
Perhaps when the chaos is done
and January 1st arrives,
I will see what I cannot see right now.

University Living

We were made of strength and stupidity.
Second-hand smoke filling the air,
drinking and singing
engulfed by the need to not care.
Midnight supermarket trips
and holding hands with misguided loves.
Stumbles and shouts
and 999 calls as a fall or a punch
lands us in hospital.
As youth runs through bones,
we risk breaking them on nights never to be forgotten
and days in the sun on the steps of campus,
drinking whiskey and rum and clinking bottles of
tequila beer.
We were free in the centre of our hearts,
led by intelligence and utter nonsense.

I would do nothing to go back
but I do miss it a lot.

Love At This Age – Inevitable

Regardless of what I say in the moment,
I will place a hand on my heart
and smile and say
unashamedly
"I will love just as hard again"

Sultry

When I cannot sleep
I have my way with words.

Christmas Cheer

It starts in the absence of snow;
that feeling of growing up reluctantly.
It is not that Christmas does not feel joyful,
rather it does not feel like Christmas as remembered.
The happiness is not because of the presents,
or of the songs and bells and once-a-year films
but of the gratitude to have lived another year.
The sadness is not because of schools not closing
but because I am accepting that people leave;
they die, they fly away or they simply just go.
It is seasonal celebrations,
but, for me, it is the yearly reflection.
The time that overwhelms;
such beauty, such pain,
such loss and such gain.

I hold Christmas in my arms with a firm grip,
and I feel it slipping away from me.
The world is changing and snow no longer falls
so predictably and the people who are still here to
wish me Happy Christmas change almost every year.

I wonder how I will feel on the day when snow falls
again on the 25th.

Will I go out and hunt for the sledge or just stay inside
and be thrown back to the nostalgia of being a child?

A Heart That Has Its Scars

I guess I am thankful for the nature of my heart
for were it not so easily infatuated,
I imagine I would have given up on love
and all its colours altogether by now.

The dastardly hopeless thing has its upsides, too.

Maturing

I would rather be filled with rage
and write page upon page of things
I need from you in order to feel better
than to still feel so much love
and know exactly nothing you can do
to make me feel better.

The Care Home Conversation Is An Old One

I want to grow old,
like we always promised we would,
together in some insufferable care home.
I want to sit and stare in reserved judgement,
making stories in our heads about Brenda
and her unashamed kleptomania.
I want to talk of old days and where we got it all
wrong.
I want to know we'll still always be there for each
other,
as we have so many times before.
I want to know this is just a small blip in our timeline
that we'll remember, laughing at how young and naive
we were.
I want to believe that we are stronger than this,
as strong as I always thought we were.
But some part of me cannot make guarantees
to my soul any longer.
Too many have lied to it before and I cannot do the
same.
The care home conversation is getting old,
and I just want someone to show me they'll stay
for the next year at least.

A Typical Week In My Twenties

I have not had the easiest of weeks.
Well, I guess that's unfair to say.
The content and context, by all accounts, have been
just fine.
The right people and the right places, just the wrong
mind.
And that's a feeling of great frustration,
to have all the right elements but just the wrong mind
or rather the right mind in a state of ill repute.
So what can one do in such situations that lend
themselves to isolation and alienation?
I could dance under the influence - let the poison take
the other and substitute its hold.
I could hide inside and pretend that time is not rapidly
passing by.
But instead, I read, I drink coffee on softly raining
evenings and I just continue.
Pain is nothing new; it has sustained my writing thus
far so it certainly has its uses.

For those days

Some days when I wake,
I hear the birds and distant chattering of early risers
and every sickly sweet thing in the world.
Some days when I wake,
I hear nothing of a honeyed disposition.
I hear the callous murmurs of a mistreated mind
and the distant silence of a maybe-future.
And yet each day,
I wake.
I wake still,
in curious anticipation,
in sanguine anxiety,
at the prospect of a morning with birds
and early risers singing together.

Pessimism.

I don't know if you could call me a pessimist or an
optimist
but i cannot help but think about the darkness in the
distance,
even when my life is full of light
and I am working on that.

Simple Solutions for Temporary Tranquillity

"I don't know what to do anymore" you say
"I cannot grasp control of my mind, I am lost and
cannot silence the noise".

"So stop trying" I say.
"Come with me, bring your favourite book,
we will sit atop the heath, when everyone else is
asleep.
I will not distract you, you can have your peace,
when we read against a blood-orange skyline.
When the blue appears to signal the day, I will kiss
your head and hold you close and it will be a new day
and you, my darling, will have survived the night."

A Prologue

In life
there is not always a happy ending,
but there is always,
without fail,
a prologue;
the memory,
the legacy,
the 5-years-later.
Focus on that.

Education

It is perhaps morbid to say so
but maybe we should stop crying
and stop praying and sending thoughts
and stop despairing
and just teach our children
a better world.

I certainly do not remember being taught in school
the things I know of the world today.

A Trip For Solitude

I have been back in England for a couple days.
I cannot say I immediately miss France, because it is
as if my brain is denying I was even there.
Still the impact of the trip is quite prominent.
The silence of a room does not hurt me quite so much.
The silence of my phone and of the friends I await
texts from does not scratch my skin as it used to.
I have found the distinction between loneliness
– the crippling disease that pains me so often -
and solitude - the thing that now brings me every
realisation I have needed to succeed.

Friends In Your Twenties

They always tell you as you grow up that you'll lose
friends along the way.
It's not until you witness it first-hand that you realise
how much of a tragedy it is.

But when you are twenty-and-some
and you see the faces that stayed,
it does not matter the specifics
- how often you see them, or what you do -
just the fact they are there means more than anything
else.

You could look them in the face in the middle of some
long awaited trip to the pub and feel the need to cry.
Not out of sadness or pain at the lost friends,
just purely out of a sweet gratitude.

The Clarity

Coffee Shop Conversations

A touch of civilisation,
a brush with the world,
connection
in contact
between others,
othered by us,
the silent ones in the corner,
with a laptop
and a coffee,
maybe a notebook,
and a hot chocolate,
maybe alone
and nervous.
The quiet rebel,
with little left
to lose,
the one that enters society,
hating it,
but wanting to be a part of it,
partially believing it is a cure for its own sins.
We are zoned in our own world,
in a bubble created by others,
sustained by us,
welcome to our mixed-up misanthropy
which is really just a cover for being afraid
of rejection or maybe worse acceptance.
We scan the room, maybe stare a little long

at the barista with the smile,
but withdraw whenever someone sits near us,
a perfect contradiction,
a broken restriction,
detailed in the wrong conversation,
or in fervent miscommunication,
we are here
to change,
it just takes time, doesn't it?
A few breaktime distances,
discovering new instances
of humanity,
screamed profanity,
when another lover leaves,
this is us,
broken and imperfect,
searching for what's worth it,
breaking our own rules,
and defining our own signs to take
the time to notice, but this is us,
coffee shop observers,
in love with the world we are so nervous of,
in love with the way love looks in public,
when people arent even trying,
in confusion with it all, learning and observing,
to encourage our own hearts to join in with the chaos.

Roots

These roots were made in damp soil and bug infested
grounds,
they were plucked and cut
until they believed they were never meant to grow,
but these roots are made from oak.
They were made to stand tall and strong
against a wave of weathers and
I am done with crying over fallen leaves in the winter.
No, I am not a fucking tree but I am grounded in roots
that will always promise to keep growing,
and I have so many reasons to smile,
least of all because I am still
growing,
alive,
showing
I have survived in the wake of so many obstacles.
I will succeed,
in believing
in my worth,
because it is what I deserve,
it is what I have worked for.
I will not stop believing
because beneath the dirt,
within the centre of my roots,
there are histories of humans
who have fought for their freedom,
there are lovers from different races

come together to create new faces,
children of conflict,
a future to predict,
a love to continue,
how can I not believe I am alive to survive
when I come from such examples of strength?
No, I have not always been so optimistic,
there have been years in dark rooms,
and locked doors with secrets hidden,
pain forgiven in replace for silence
so that others may not arrive at a conclusion
that I need help because I already knew I did,
but a childhood of conflict, contradicted my ability to
trust.
But this is why I will not stop believing,
because I have been a young boy
in a room full of toys and doll houses,
being asked what it was like.
I have been too old too young,
and had crayons placed in my hands
to draw what I thought was going on in my mind,
but this is why I will not stop believing.
Because my life hasn't always been so much
happiness.
Now there are the times when everything is calmer,
when I can share a laugh, and ask someone to be a
friend knowing they will never stop until we are dead,
the times when I can stop, and look at the past
knowing that the times I thought could never last did

and the trauma I thought would never stop hurting,
did.
You see life likes to sneak up on you,
sometimes with a vengeance,
and other times with a guidance.
Guiding others has also been a reason for me
to never give up,
and this is why I will not stop believing,
because if I can take my life,
and turn it around,
take my mind,
and make sense of it,
then maybe I can teach others to do the same.
Inspire a fire in the hearts of broken humans
searching for a new self to be, a new life to see beyond
the past.

I will not stop believing in dreams and miracles,
because they are just realities given a chance,
given patience,
given time.

Sleepless Sunday Optimism

We could sail away and make our great escape,
Throw out the oars and drift along the tide
Or we could jump off the side and float to the bottom,
Kiss the seabed and search its metropolis.
Imagine if the sun met the moon at the arrival of night.
Imagine it stayed.
Imagine the amber white colouring the land.
The unlikely pair would shine down on the earth,
reach through to minds unfiltered and ask
"Don't you ever wonder what's beyond the silver
shimmer?"
And I don't know about you but I would shed a tear
watching the rain hit the ocean,
With a hint of the shore ever clearer, gleaming in the
distance, pining for attention,
wondering if I could still make it to that hint on the
horizon without drowning.
And just imagine if it was possible,
if heads were kept above water
until feet shuffled onto shore,
No more roads burning or leaves fallen red,
just a chance taken,
and the roots of trees spreading across the soil below,
and the greens of its leaves stretching out to the sky
above.
Just imagine that. Just imagine the glow.

Not Fading

It's hard when these emotions last,
but even when a part of you lies in the past,
life moves so fast that you'd never have such a
beautiful heart without the harsh
half of your staccato start,
so don't forget that.
It's a strange arrangement when your world
is moving forward into an unfurled existence
and all you see is distance and dissonance,
this is a conflict, I get it,
and I know you're bored of all the "dont sweat it's"
but really its just a yearly battle through the seasons,
and when you are rattling the cage to list all the
reasons why you're failing,
listen to your heart racing,
it's still not fading,
so you must be sailing some sort of
course in the right direction
and anyway, protection against pain
is like avoiding the rain by staying inside, it still
arrives,
so grab a coat and test the waters.

Pride

I never gave enough time to the idea of pride.
Not the type to hit a mother watching her son at his
first performance, or seeing him ride his bike but the
type of pride that lies inside the body and keeps us
stubborn.
The one that tries so hard to impress,
the complex mess of depression and excessive people
pleasing tendencies.
A different type of pride.
A bad one.
The one that takes the pain and finds a way to make it
ten times worse.
The one that cannot accept when it is wrong until it is
home and time to cry.
The one that cuts us deep and refuses our small request
to sleep.
The one that rises up and asks in knowing tones
"Are you going to stop me this time?"
And I have begun to answer Yes and oh what a
difference it makes to defy just one time.

In Hindsight

I have been thinking recently
that perhaps things were never that simple.
And that somewhere down below the gut of such
stubborn emotion
I always knew that.
I could see when something was going to be worth it.
I could see when something was going to crash and
burn.
And yet, whether out of infatuation or out of
resentment, i refused to accept either eventuality.
So it leads to a point where i look back on so many
situations in my past now that have made me who i am
today with no resentment or sadness
but a refreshed realisation of the facts.
Like it took getting just that little bit older
to start to piece together the few remaining pieces.
This is who I was,
this is who they were
and whether that is still true now is,
to some extent, irrelevant.
There are some patches on the heart that are peeled
back to still reveal the open wound,
and others that are cleanly healed.
Some will never change and that is okay.
Of course, I still feel uncontrollable sadness
and even as I write this,
I am unsure of what the future holds.

I know I am passionate and driven
but I am also desperately pained and that,
I have accepted will never change.
But I have found ways to improve my quality of life,
and much of that is being able to look back and,
whether unfortunate or otherwise,
see in a much simpler clarity of thought
the beauty and the pain.
She loved me in one way
and then she loved me in another
and i think, somewhere along the way,
I was unsure which reality of feeling i wanted
or needed to be true.
Or in fact, perhaps more realistically,
if i needed either to be true.
I loved both in different ways
and i forged the truth far too many times for me to
understand what was real or not.
But now i think i understand a little clearer that
neither was black or white or simple
and it makes no sense to try and pretend they were.
And both make no sense to see as anything other
than fading film in an old Pentax.

Dear Self - What does it matter?

There comes a moment when everything appears to have gone wrong.

You lay upon your bed, the sheets creased and dusty, the floor of the room equally as messy and cluttered from where the depression has sunken in and stolen all care you had for cleanliness.

You play some depressing playlist and sing along like this whole fucking world is a music video about heartbreak and you stay as far away from any couple as you can.

But you're not bitter and you're not really anti-love.

You're inherently romantic and you still appreciate the smiles on peoples faces lighting up when a text crosses their phone screen.

But you begin to look back on your life like a series of failed sitcoms.

You investigate each 'almost' and wonder if you had just missed out on the wrong people; if you never actually loved anyone.

You felt something because it was there, for sure.

You used to see their pictures and think they were the
grace of the earth.
You felt the momentary silences in between sentences
where you wondered if they would tell you the
words you were looking for.
But they didn't come, and even when your words did,
were you ever really sure?
Is the doubt even real? Or just a mechanism designed
to heal your heart from all the fallen loves.
Well, here's my feeling, if you care to listen:
'In Love' is questionable, but I think it always will be.
What is true is that you felt so truly for them
(those your mind have flickered toward over the years)
and they, at least, cared for you; you cannot deny that.
So then, with that in mind,
what do the specificities matter?
What care should you give to remembering where
your love lied?
In their heart?
In their eyes?
In the surprise of your ultimate demise?
Do not worry your mind with it all.
It's all juvenile now.
No, you're wrong, it would not be closure, it would
only open the wound further.

Listen, whatever the circumstances may have been
or may still be, you were lucky to feel something.
When they glanced at you a little too long, and you felt

that strong feeling of being wanted,
you became anew.

When they rested their head against your shoulder
when everything was heavy,
you became anew.

When they called you beautiful or told you they loved
you or called you just to hear your voice,
you became anew.

And look at you now:

You are so new and ready to chose your path in life
and whomever enters and becomes your partner or
whatever,
they will have met you as a product of all these
feelings.
As you became anew, you grew.

So what does it matter?

Myths of Childhood

Bus rides to school, often offered mint humbugs by
some overly social stranger.
Best friends for life promised in a tight pact or
bracelet.
A trip to the chip shop at lunchtime, chewy
fried egg sweets and smarties brought with any small
change found between the sofas sides.

Just a small snapshot of my British adolescence
defined by countryside living.
But more than the normal routines,
the niche habits of me and my friends,
we were all conditioned to believe specific things.

We were taught to believe we had to be a certain way.
We had to go at a certain pace;
Virginity lost by 18.
The 'key to the house' at 21.
Engaged or married at 24 and at least a baby by 26.

As men, we could be not be 'frigid' or rigid with our
masculinity, we had to fight and fuck like a stud.
As women, they could not be promiscuous or
passionate, they had to study and socialise in
moderation unlike the 'sluts'.

Toxic systemic conditions

we did not realise we were
living under the influence of.
Let me break a few down
and list the truths for the youths still unaware:
Sex is not as black and white as it made it to be.

Virginity is not a shameful thing, it is a concept.

Loving sex and having a lot of it is not a shameful
thing either.

Whatever your preference,
whatever your pace,
whatever your pleasure,
if no-one is hurt and
everything is consensual,
it is what you make it.

Timing is subjective.
Do things when they are comfortable for you,
plan your life or don't.

Be 27 and have nothing structured so long as you are
happy.
Be 35 with no kids and no marriage and no care in the
world.
Be 20 with a good job, but less of a social life and be
proud of your choice.
Be 56 and change your entire life with no regrets.

Be you.

Tolerance is mandatory.
Understand the people around you.
Learn what you were never taught.
Talk to people you do not comprehend.
Do not be the stubborn one that shouts abuse without
context.

Be kind to others and to yourself and do not live under
the pressure of anyone else's timing.

Love 2.0

Embers ashes
have been fashioned into passionate
love that lies behind my ribs.
I used to let it flutter and scratch but now it causes a
ruckus and lacks the patience of a child that does not
know its worth.
It is a bold bravery that knows when to leave and when
to stay.
It is a feeling that wraps me in a faux fur coat for
warmth and asks if I need shelter.
It is the thing I have not treated properly,
I have berated and abused,
It is the love that I must amuse
to believe it exists.

How to change the world.

Do your research.
Educate yourself.
Craft your means of expression.
Then educate the world into an acceptance of a grand
tolerance in replace of conditioned systemic
inequalities of social and financial exclusion and
remember your fight may feel tiresome but it is
worthy.
We are naturally told to keep our most passionate,
divisive thoughts to ourselves yet that never seems to
apply to the most toxic, world-damaging, socially
traditional values that are routinely screamed from
bigoted rooftops.

First, understand that feeling the need to do something
about inequality and injustice becomes a purpose.

Once that purpose has been defined,
it is a scratch that does not leave.
It is a passion and a creative necessity that demands
action.
If you feel that grab within the gut that can only be
solved by expressing such views and finding a way to
improve flawed sections of our world,
do not be shamed into submission.
Put in the work.
Be open-minded.

Have healthy discussions and fight harder.
Forget the myths that being so politically and socially
vocal makes us less attractive
it is, and always has been,
a myth made in fear of change.

Be independent.
Be passionate.
Be whatever or whoever
you chose to be and be picky
about who your care to keep as company.

Duty

Our only true duty in life
is to find what makes our heart sing
and not let it go,
even if that means
some temporary pain.

I like Adulthood, actually.

I don't need the status.
I don't care for the riches.
I don't mind if I am not liked
by the more popular kids.
I don't need validation.
I don't see myself as unworthy of care.
This is not school any more,
this is adulthood
and as painful as it feels sometimes,
it will always be better
than the social strain of school without restraint.

Old Friends.

We're not the weekly meetups.
We're not the regular calls.
We're not the pub trips at nightime
at a minutes notice.
We are the lengthy catchups.
We are the nostalgia every time.
We are the growing happiness.
We are the maturity of new freedom.
We are old friends with new lives
and that is just as beautiful
because we have seen our individual evolution.

In Spirit

When my breathing stops
and my heart begins to fight,
I have begun to turn to the sky
and find peace.

Where do you see yourself?

I want to spend the next 5 years
proving every lie I ever told myself wrong
with each new revelation of excellence.

Regret?

I don't know if it is what I needed,
nor if I would be so brazen to say
that I would not go back if I could
but one thing I do know
is that it has made
all the difference
- for better, for worse.

Soon

I'm excited for who we will grow to be.

Realisation.

I don't think I love you any more
but I did once,
it's true, I did.
It hurt like the best of them
and healed unlike the rest of them.
And I feel I have been both the flower
and the water and even the fox that came to chew
when I was loving you,
I was growing beside the seed I would become
and perhaps the old soil is something that I miss
but I have learnt from the wilting
and I am not mad at the death
but I may leave a lily to gaze upon
as I love another.

Better

Sunrise, when time flies
and speakers are loud,
allowed to care less
but we still sneak it in,
like chocolate in a diet,
or customised uniforms at school,
you see the winter is fading,
our ship is sailing,
and I am ready for the future,
you might think this is just an effect
of the oncoming summer,
and the spring is the spring in my step,
with a tan and longer evenings,
of course I'm going to be happy,
but this is different, my friend,
this is no maybe,
this is certain,
the curtains are drawn,
and I wake up in the morning,
with a single yawn
and a stretch to the ceiling,
knowing I am healing
the wounds of the past,
that were never meant to last so long.
You thought I would be
just another b grade human,
no time to be remade

into a home-made success,
nothing less than a broken boy from a broken home
but let me just correct you there,
I was never going to be,
the broken boy you used to see
around the town, head down,
avoiding the crowd.
Now lets remember that boy,
no normal kid with his toys,
but an anger and a scream,
now a man with a plan,
and a need to live his dream.
Dont underestimate that,
because a broken boy
is now a man who sees the beauty in the everyday.
People used to say its better to stay away from him,
or better still make the drops on his cheeks wetter still,
and now look at him
working everyday
to pay to pave his way to the top,
this is not going to stop,
I am finding new words every morning
to describe my feelings and that is all I ever needed,
care, and love, and a platform to thrive,
patience and time and a shit load of drive
this is not going to stop,
because I used to care what others thought,
but here's one thing pain and trauma has taught
me,

there's always someone with a problem with you,
but the problem is when you can't care for yourself,
selfishness is not always a sin,
and caring for others does not always heal within,
so I am trying to redefine my design
to come out better
so hold my hand, and come with me,
we'll be old and stand beside the sea,
knowing we fought the tide,
and stung the bee,
and left singing under the willow tree,
we are better than anyone could have expected.

To Exist

You give me a reason to exist, even when it hurts to.

New

I open my eyes
and wake to see
who I will be
in this new
regeneration of me.

Simply Unsimple

The answer is always
to keep living
and let life suprise you.

Accepting Myself

It will take a special kind of person to love me
because they will have to love all of me
and even I can't do that.
I am the forest but I am also the buried bodies
and the foxes that hunt.
I am the sweetness of candy floss
but also the decay that rots the teeth.
I am the Friday feeling and I am the Monday morning.
I am the mood swings.
I am the Anxiety.
I am the Depression.
And I lied at the beginning of this poem
because I *do* love all of me
and a person does not have to be a special kind,
they just have to be human
and be patient
and understand that if I love them,
I will at some point doubt their love for me.
It is wired into this often tired brain,
it is the pain speeding down the fast lane,
it is the angry commuter
hurrying up the left side of the escalator,
it is the pen without ink.
It is my blood
and I am working on working with it
but it is not an easy colleague.
It leaves its mess everywhere

and it does not tell me when it has
a great new fucking idea,
it just runs with it and leaves me
with the mess and tears and then rears its head
when I am just lying peacefully in bed.

"Fuck off" I tell it
and take the time to watch its shock
and somehow it still hurts me
to see its sadness.
I am not me and it,
we are the same
so the only way to change
is to change with him
and as long as that might take
I am willing to make the effort.

Futures

I think I might stop building futures with friends and
crushes
and only promise what I have the control to deliver:
The future with myself.

Progress

To sit in a room with myself
and not hate the silence
is to celebrate.

Its the small things

Some moments seem typically romantic of a writers
fantasy but they are just so magically true.
Like the moment just now
sat at my desk in the heart of
a British winter with the wind of a passing storm
barging against the window.
I pen journals of a difficult week against my
cream lined paper
- the notepad with the broken bind –
with Ray on the speakers singing of the best thing.
Then the little light that beams in and is gone before I
can capture it.

Fantasy though it may feel,
it is the real, small things that deserve to be
in every novel of beautiful things.

As I get older

It troubles me how easily things change
upon changing my outlook.
Yet here we are
with the word "yes"
being uttered more often than ever before.

This, to all:

I have a selection of letters,
each with different headers
and a name to every one
but this, to all:
I have loved and lost
and I am sorry for the hurt.
I have been a different man
across many chapters
and through all I have made mistakes.
But I wake every day
and think of new ways
to let love win
and to know when
one thing is worthy
and another is not.

Journaling as an adult.

It has been a while since I wrote a journal entry.
But here I am.
A lot has changed since I last opened this book to talk.
Revelations and epiphanies and such.
More than anything, i think I'm getting used to my age
and all the confusions that come with it.
The fact I miss my old job is quite possibly one of the
strangest realisations yet.
But here's why its a thing.
It represented a pivotal chapter in my life.
I was growing and,
begrudgingly,
owe a lot to that time.
And it was like school or college, again,
neither of which I enjoyed but both of which came
with intense bonds and relationships.
The job was the same with just as much drama.
But I am seeing its benefits now
and that realisation is the perfect example of how I
feel about growing older as the days pass by so
quickly.
Though I have memories to take with me,
I am changing into a different version of me,
perhaps every 5 years or so.
Whether I am completely void of responsibility,
or dredged under rent and council tax
or whatever the bloody hell saving ISA's are,

the same will always be true.
I will feel what I am feeling at the time,
I will be scared
or excited
or emotional
but at some point,
the hands will change.
The conditions will improve or falter,
I will go through ups and downs
and there is no way, through control or will,
to predict if the path I walk will be the one I wish for,
but there will always be a "5 months later"
or even a "5 years later".
There will be me suddenly missing the moments that
broke my heart, not for the actual breaking
or the people that broke it,
but for the cracks in between that I could not see,
for the happiness, the laughter, the healing that carried
on in the background.

It is always there.
However long it takes me to see it.
And til my dying day,
I will wait through the pain,
to see it again and again.

We All Die.

Until recently I feared death
like it was the man and the scythe himself
haunting me at every corner
and not just the prospect
of the silent emptiness.
I could not envision what came before me
and I could not imagine my life
simply ceasing to exist;
a momentary mark on history
like a billion others
and then the sudden darkness.
I would stay awake at night
staring at the ceiling and seeing the universe,
as it would be without me,
and I questioned often
whether it ever actually mattered that I was there.
But with the years, as they have evolved,
and with so many close shaves to an early grave,
I am starting to lose the fear.
I fear more the waste of a life obsessed with it.
You see,
I do not know if there is an 'after' or a 'before'.
I know we are here and I believe,
however many people live on this earth,
however many lives may coexist,
we have a touch on time.
We effect our surroundings,

we impact the progression of life,
we step foot on new grounds
and teach our children to sing.
Whatever reason our universe is here,
we are in it to make it a better place.
We have lived through great tragedies
and we have born terrible tyrants,
but we are each here with a chance to impact
something.
Whether it is the lives of those around us,
equally questioning their purpose on the planet,
or whether it is something larger.
Whether we are meant to be leaders or followers
or some medium in between,
we impact something
and much like everything,
none of it would be so sweet
or so important
if there was no end.

Thank You For Reading!

Thank you for reading my 2nd collection of poetry and prose. I have been putting this together pretty much since I released my debut collection Whispers To The World. This self-publishing business is a complicated one and comes with its pros and its cons, but it is a truly beautiful thing to share my work with whoever is reading this now, and to connect with so many of the souls I have over the years.

If this is the first time you've ever heard of me, welcome to the gang, first of all! We're a nice bunch. I'm a British writer from Caribbean descent who spends most of his time drowning in cups of tea and coffee, and writing for publications such as Thought Catalog and The Mighty. I publish poetry on my Instagram @liamxavierwrites and you can also find me as a book reviewer at Reedsy Discovery. I am almost never satisfied, so you will always find me doing a multitude of things, but I am a writer before anything else. While I grew up in Essex, I now reside in London where you can catch me at spoken word events, and putting on theatre shows with one of my best friends through Wilflen Theatre.
Feel free to reach out if anything in particular resonated with you or you have any questions about the self publishing journey, I'd love to chat!

9 781838 027100